Inspector's Manual

Halal Monitoring Authority
Canada

For the concern of genuine halal

Inspector's Manual

Halal Monitoring Authority
Canada

Acknowledgments:

HMA Board
Shaykh Omar Subedar

Designed and Printed in 2017

Halal Monitoring Authority
www.HMACanada.org

Index

1. Who is the Halal Monitoring Authority?... 1
2. What is the definition of Halal?... 2
3. What is the definition of Haram? 3
4. Why is a halal diet important?... 4
5. What are the names and definitions of facilities in the food industry?............... 6
6. What is an HMA Inspector?... 6
7. What does an HMA Inspector do at a poultry abattoir?..................................... 7
8. What does an HMA Inspector do at a red meats abattoir?................................ 8
9. What does an HMA Inspector do at a processing plant?................................... 9
10. What does an HMA Inspector do at a butcher shop?....................................... 10
11. What does an HMA Inspector do at a restaurant? 11
12. How is an HMA inspector to behave?.. 12
13. What are the safety rules tied with an inspector's role?................................... 13
14. Why is the role of an HMA inspector so important?... 13

Who is the Halal Monitoring Authority?

Introduction

The Halal Monitoring Authority (HMA) is a department of the Canadian Council of Muslim Theologians (CCMT). The CCMT is a non-for profit organization registered in Canada.

Objectives

To monitor halal labelled products from production to retail in order to save the halal customer from being fooled.

History

In 2004, a person from the halal industry complained to the CCMT about malpractices in the halal meat market. Haram was being sold in the name of halal. The person demanded that the CCMT members do something to stop this. To first understand the market, the CCMT appointed a team. This team managed to inspect 13 poultry abattoirs, 4 red meat abattoirs and 7 processing plants. Throughout these inspections, which were all documented, the team discovered the following areas of concern:

1- Muslim slaughter men at abattoirs were not reciting bismillah during slaughter
2- Non-Muslims were being used to slaughter halal animals at some abattoirs
3- The minimum number of veins and pipes were not being cut properly
4- Animals were being stunned before slaughter
5- Poultry was being slaughtered by a mechanical blade.
6- Meat distributors were cheating butcher stores and restaurants by selling haram meat to them in the name of halal.
7- Retailers had no idea where their meat was really coming from.
8- Imported meat was being labeled and sold as halal.

This was all reported the Directors of the CCMT. The CCMT was then introduced to a monitoring committee in the UK called the Halal Monitoring Committee. It decided to send a delegation to them to learn their system. The delegation made a visit, and upon their return, the CCMT established a new department called the Halal Monitoring Authority. By the grace of Allah, this department has been operating successfully ever since.

Inspector's Manual – HMA

What is Halal?

Halal in Arabic means "allowed" or "permissible." Technically, it is a title given to everything we as Muslims are allowed to use or do.

When it comes to food, a Muslim may eat non-vegetarian food as long as the following conditions are met:

1. The food is sourced from the following animals:

   - Poultry and domestic birds
   - Cattle
   - Sheep and goats
   - Camels
   - Buck
   - Rabbits
   - Fish
   - Locusts

2. With the exception of fish and locusts, the animals must be slaughtered in the following manner:

   - The slaughter-man is Muslim.
   - He recites, "Bismillah," or "Bismillahi Allahu Akbar," at the time of slaughter.
   - The animal is alive at the time of slaughter.
   - Using a sharp knife, the slaughter-man completely cuts the two jugular veins of the animal manually along with its trachea and esophagus. Mechanical slaughter is unacceptable. If cutting all four is not possible then cutting any three of the four will suffice.
   - He does the cut in one motion rather than multiple ones.

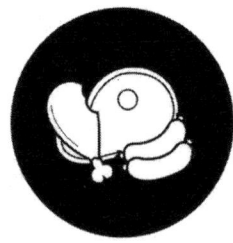

What is Haram?

Haram in Arabic means "not allowed" or "impermissible." Technically, it is a title given to everything we as Muslims are not allowed to use or do.

When it comes to food, a Muslim cannot eat the following items:

- Any animal fit for Muslim consumption that was not slaughtered according to the slaughter guidelines mentioned above.
- Pork and pork products
- Carnivores
- Reptiles
- Insects excluding locusts
- Intoxicants ex. alcohol, recreational drugs etc.
- Blood
- Ingredients derived from any of the items mentioned on this list

Why is a Halal Diet Important?

Keeping a halal diet is important because Allah has ordered it:

1. "Messengers, eat of good foods, and do good deeds." (Surat al-Mu'minūn 23:51)
2. "You who believe, eat of the good things we have provided you [...]." (Surat al-Baqarah 2:172)
3. "Mankind, eat of the things in the land that is lawful and good." (Surat al-Baqarah 2:168)
4. "So, eat of that (meat) upon which Allah's name was mentioned, if you believe in His verses." (Surat al-An'am 6:118)
5. "And do not eat whatever Allah's name was not taken on, for indeed, it is a grave disobedience." (Surat al-An'am 6:121)

If a person fails to practise a halal diet:

1. Their prayers (du'as) will not be accepted:

   Abu Hurayrah reported, "Allah's Messenger (peace be upon him) said, 'Indeed, Allah is good, and He only accepts what is good. Allah has given those orders to the believers, which he has given to the Messengers. He stated, "Messengers, eat of good foods, and do good deeds." He [also] stated, "You who believe, eat of the good things we have provided you [...].'"
   The Prophet (peace be upon him) then made mention of a man who undergoes a long journey disheveled and dusty. He spreads his hands towards the sky (calling), 'My Rabb, my Rabb.' However, his food is haram, his drink is haram, his clothes are haram, and he has been nourished with haram! So how will his call be answered?" (Sahih Muslim)

2. Their good deeds will be rejected for 40 days:

   Sa'd reported, "Allah's messenger (peace be upon him) said, 'Sa'd purify your food. [As a result,] you will become one who's prayers are accepted. I swear by He in whose hands the soul of Muhammad lies, [whenever] a servant [of Allah] tosses a haram morsel into their stomach, no deed is accepted from them for 40 days.'" (Mu'jam al-Tabarani)

3. They will not enter Jannah:

    Abu Bakr narrated that Allah's Messenger (peace be upon him) said, "A body that has been nourished with haram will not enter Paradise." (Bayhaqi)

    Jabir reported, "Allah's Messenger (peace be upon him) said, 'That flesh will not enter Paradise which has grown from haram. Every flesh that is grown from haram, the Fire [of Jahannam] is more worthy of it.'" (Bayhaqi)

What Are the Names and Definitions of Facilities in the Food Industry?

Abattoir: A facility where animals are slaughtered. Those that are monitored by the Canadian Food Inspection Agency (CFIA) are called federal plants. Those that are monitored by the Ontario Ministry of Agriculture, Food and Rural Affairs (OMAFRA) are called provincial plants.

Processing Plant: A place where meat is deboned, cut, cooked or made into finished food products ex. strips, patties, nuggets, kebabs etc.

Butcher Shop: A store that sells fresh meat and meat products to the general public.

Restaurant: A place where people order food and dine.

What is an HMA Inspector?

An HMA Inspector is a person who monitors the production and storage of halal food throughout various parts of the food production chain. They ensure that at every stage, HMA halal guidelines are completely met.

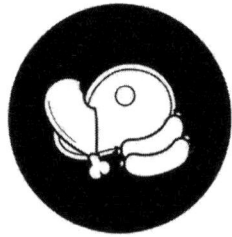

What does an HMA Inspector do at a Poultry Abattoir?

An HMA inspector is to:

1. Report their time of arrival at the facility on the HMA Inspectors Hub group on WhatsApp.
2. Make sure that all equipment and production lines are completely washed and sanitized before the HMA production begins.
3. Make sure that all non-Halal products have been segregated in the coolers and in the operation areas before HMA operations begin, so that no contamination between halal and haram products occur.
4. Check the voltage of the stunner and make sure it is within the acceptable limit. Kindly check the abattoir instruction sheet for the specific voltage.
5. Make sure that the slaughter-man is Muslim, and is alert.
6. Make sure that the slaughter-man visibly pronounces bismillah by moving their lips upon each bird during slaughter.
7. Make sure that the slaughter-men do not talk amongst themselves while slaughtering.
8. Make sure that the slaughter-men completely cut (1) the esophagus, (2) the trachea, and (3) the two jugular veins when slaughtering the bird. If for some reason, completely cutting all four is not possible, they must completely cut at least three of the aforementioned four.
9. Make sure that there are a sufficient number of slaughter-men to carry out the slaughter comfortably. The instruction sheet specific to the abattoir will dictate the proper number for the operation.
10. Make sure that there are an adequate number of spare knives throughout the operation.
11. Make sure that the water temperature for scalder does not go over 60C°/ 140 f.
12. Report all infractions and incidents of concern to the head inspectorate immediately.
13. Fill all the necessary fields on the cloud upon completing the inspection.
14. Report their time of departure from the facility on the HMA Inspectors Hub group on WhatsApp.

What does an HMA Inspector do at a Red Meats Abattoir?

An HMA inspector is to:

1. Report their time of arrival at the facility on the HMA Inspectors Hub group on WhatsApp.
2. Make sure that all equipment and production lines are completely washed and sanitized before the HMA production begins.
3. Make sure that all non-Halal products have been segregated in the coolers and in the operation areas before HMA operations begin, so that no contamination between halal and haram products occur.
4. Make sure that no stunning equipment is used at all unless authorized by the head office.
5. Make sure that the slaughter-man is Muslim and not under the influence.
6. Make sure that the slaughter-man visibly pronounces bismillah by moving their lips upon each animal during slaughter.
7. Make sure that the slaughter-man does not talk with someone else while slaughtering.
8. Make sure that the slaughter-man completely cuts (1) the esophagus, (2) the trachea, and (3) the two jugular veins when slaughtering an animal. If for some reason, completely cutting all four is not possible, they must completely cut at least three of the aforementioned four.
9. Stamp approved carcasses in the areas identified by the head inspectorate.
10. Mark unapproved carcasses with the marker provided, and arrange for it to be segregated.
11. Report all infractions and incidents of concern to the head inspectorate immediately.
12. Fill all the necessary fields on the cloud upon completing the inspection.
13. Report their time of departure from the facility on the HMA Inspectors Hub group on WhatsApp.

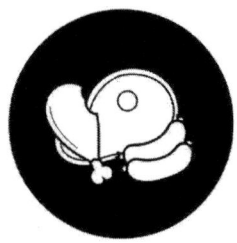

What does an HMA Inspector do at a Processing Plant?

An HMA inspector is to:

1. Report their time of arrival at the facility on the HMA Inspectors Hub group on WhatsApp.
2. Make sure that all equipment and production lines are completely washed and sanitized before the HMA production begins.
3. Make sure that all non-Halal products have been segregated in the storage areas and in the operation areas before HMA operations begin, so that no contamination between halal and haram products occur.
4. Identify the meat to be processed by checking the required stamps, labels and tags, and then check the HMA cloud to ensure that all the information is accurate and consistent.
5. Remain on the production line, once production begins, to ensure that only HMA certified meat is processed throughout the assigned times.
6. Stamp boxes with an HMA date stamp, or tie bags with HMA tape once production is complete.
7. Report all infractions and incidents of concern to the head inspectorate immediately.
8. Fill in all the necessary fields on the cloud upon completing the inspection.
9. Report their time of departure from the facility on the HMA Inspectors Hub group on WhatsApp.

Inspector's Manual – HMA

What does an HMA Inspector do at a Butcher Shop?

An HMA inspector is to:

1. Make regular visits to the certified retailer to check if HMA guidelines are being met.
2. Report their time of visit at the store on the HMA Store Inspectors Hub group on WhatsApp.
3. Make sure that the HMA certificate is in a place that is clear and readable for the customer.
4. Make sure that HMA dividers are properly placed in the meat display.
5. Make sure that non-HMA certified meat is not present, unless authorized by the head inspectorate.
6. Count the number of boxed products and fresh meats in the coolers, and freezers if need be, and make sure that the numbers are consistent with what is recorded in the cloud.
7. Check invoices, if foul play is suspected.
8. If non-HMA certified meats are found, instruct the store owner or manager to segregate them and make arrangements to return them. Report this infraction to the head inspectorate immediately. The head inspectorate will correspond with the store owner or manager. He will issue further instructions on the course of action to be taken, thereafter.
9. Remove the certificate from the site, when instructed by the head inspectorate to do so.

Inspector's Manual – HMA

What does an HMA Inspector do at a Restaurant?

1. Make regular visits to the certified outlet to check if HMA guidelines are being met.
2. Make sure that all changes to the menu are reported to the head inspectorate.
3. Make sure that non-HMA certified meat is not present, unless authorized by the head inspectorate.
4. Count the number of boxed products and fresh meats in the coolers, and freezers if need be, and make sure that the numbers are consistent with what is recorded in the cloud.
5. Go through the ingredients and products list, and make sure the items onsite are consistent with the list.
6. Check invoices, if foul play is suspected.
7. If non-HMA certified items are found, instruct the store owner or manager to remove them without delay. Report this infraction to the head inspectorate immediately. The head inspectorate will correspond with the restaurant owner or manager. He will issue further instructions on the course of action to be taken, thereafter.
8. Remove the certificate from the outlet, when instructed by the head inspectorate to do so.

How is an HMA Inspector to behave?

- Abide by the terms set out in your contract.
- Always arrive at the facility enough time before the production that allows you to comfortably get ready.
- Wear clean clothes at all times and be presentable.
- Abide by the rules of the facility at all times.
- Smile upon arriving at the facility. Be a source of happiness for everyone onsite. Be friendly and courteous with employees and employers. Respect older workers.
- Keep all information confidential. Do not disclose it to anyone except the HMA head inspectorate.
- Ensure that no HMA equipment (stamp, tapes, etc.) is left behind on-site, once your job is finished.
- Remember that you are employed by HMA and not the abattoirs or plants. Hence, only take operational instructions from the head inspectorate.
- Submit "Absence of Leave Form" to the head inspectorate, and get it approved prior to taking any time off.
- Contact head inspectorate for any emergencies that require you to not be on the job.
- Do not engage in any halal debate with any person onsite. Provide the email info@hmacanada.org to a concerned person for them to direct their concerns.
- Try and provide help to workers, where you are allowed to by the facility. Show them that you are there to assist them, not police them.
- Work cautiously vigilantly and wisely. Contact the head inspectorate if any operational issue arises.
- Do not accept or give money or gifts without prior authorization from the head inspectorate.

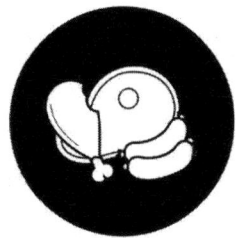

What are the Safety Rules tied with an Inspector's role?

- Always have safety boots / shoes on, hair / beard net on, overcoat, and helmet (if required) when in the kill area or processing area.
- Wash both hands when entering the processing area and after using the washroom.
- Use the footbaths if they are installed.
- Do not chew gum or tobacco at the facility.
- Do not sneeze or blow your nose without covering your mouth.
- Ensure that the area you are in is not hazardous to your safety and health.
- Report all safety concerns to the plant manager. If no action is taken, contact the head inspectorate immediately.

Why is the role of an HMA Inspector so important?

Being an HMA inspector is an incredible responsibility. It is not like your average 9 to 5 job. Rather, it is a responsibility that when done properly, carries tremendous rewards. If it is neglected, there will be severe consequences in the hereafter. This can be better understood through the following hadith:

The Prophet (peace be upon him) said, "Whosoever introduces a good practice in Islam, they will receive its reward and the reward of those who act upon it after them without anything being diminished from their rewards. And whosoever introduces an evil practice in Islam, will shoulder its sin and the sins of all those who will act upon it, without diminishing their burden in any way". (Sahih Muslim)

As an HMA representative, you are providing the public the assurance that what they are receiving is an uncompromised, genuine halal product. This assurance can only be credible if we carry out our responsibilities properly.

Made in the USA
Columbia, SC
22 April 2024